CONTENTS

Photo credits: All photos by Vince Serbin unless otherwise credited. Front endpapers of a friendly Mynah perched on a finger by Sam Fehrenz. Back endpapers show a rare breeding pair of Mynahs by Sam Fehrenz. Title page: "Karen with her Mynah" by Dr. Herbert R. Axelrod.

y T.F.H. Publications,

ISBN 0-87666-890-2

Distributed in the UNITED STATES by T.F.H. Publications, Inc., 211 West Sylvania Avenue, Neptune City, NJ 07753; in CANADA by H & L Pet Supplies Inc., 27 Kingston Crescent, Kitchener, Ontario N2B 2T6; Rolf C. Hagen Ltd., 3225 Sartelon Street, Montreal 382 Quebec; in ENGLAND by T.F.H. Publications Limited, 4 Kier Park, Ascot, Berkshire SL5 7DS; in AUSTRALIA AND THE SOUTH PACIFIC by T.F.H. (Australia) Pty. Ltd., Box 149, Brookvale 2100 N.S.W., Australia; in NEW ZEALAND by Ross Haines & Son, Ltd., 18 Monmouth Street, Grey Lynn, Auckland 2 New Zealand; in SINGAPORE AND MALAYSIA by MPH Distributors Pte., 71-77 Stamford Road, Singapore 0617; in the PHILIPPINES by Bio-Research, 5 Lippay Street, San Lorenzo Village, Makati, Rizal; in SOUTH AFRICA by Multipet Pty. Ltd., 30 Turners Avenue, Durban 4001. Published by T.F.H. Publications Inc., Ltd., the British Crown Colony of Hong Kong. THIS IS THE 1983 EDITION.

MYNAHS

MARTIN WEIL

Introduction

A pair of Gray-headed Starlings, above. Photo by Walsrode Vogelpark. In the photo to the right, a Mynah's claws automatically clench when it is held upside down. Though it is biting the model's hand, it does not have enough strength to hurt.

If man is dust in the wind, then a bird is dust on the wing.

Singing dust.

A bird is a winged singer.

That is, if it is a member of the order Passeriformes. The order of Passerine birds, writes Peter Hutchinson, is "an order containing more than a third of all living families and over half the living bird species. The Passerines are the so-called perching birds and have feet adapted to cling to branches, reeds or even man-made objects such as telephone wires in such a way that the grip automatically tightens when the bird falls backwards. Passerines include

all those birds noted for their ability to sing, and are sometimes called the 'song birds' as a result."

Birds are more ancient than man. On the Fifth Day God created "fowl that may fly above the earth in the open firmament of heaven." Man did not appear until the Sixth Day. Nonetheless, man is given dominion over the fowl of the air.

In modern days, when the ancient intimacy of man with nature has been sundered by industrial civilization, this dominion is most commonly exercised by a visit to a neighborhood pet shop. By caring for and raising a baby bird to adulthood, a young person can experience the responsibility and happiness that Adam first had.

It is often argued that to cage a bird is to destroy its happiness, and it is clear that an irresponsible owner can bring great misery to a captive bird. On the other hand, however, the power granted to man to rule over birds can be seen more as a test of man's faithfulness than as an inevitable diminution of a bird's natural liberty and contentment. If man is meant to rule over birds, then surely a bird is meant to benefit by submitting to the dominion of its master. The challenge to a pet owner is to transform an initially awkward and somewhat suspicious relationship into a lasting natural bond of affection and trust.

Birds can be very beautiful in the wild. "They often gather in spectacular numbers to roost at night," writes Oliver L. Austin, Jr. of the wild Mynah Bird. "Just before going to roost, and again at dawn, the flocks climb high into the air and execute a series of mass evolutions. Wheeling and turning in unison with almost military precision, the birds course back and forth in tremendous tittering swarms before settling down for the night or scattering for the day's foraging." There is no room in such a scene for man except as an awed observer.

In his Foreword to Boosey's *Foreign Bird Keeping,* the Rt. Hon. The Viscount Chaplin offers these sane observations.

"For thousands of years many kinds of birds large and small have willingly or unwillingly shared men's abodes. If it is doubtful what benefit this association has bestowed on birds it is certain that both aesthetically and practically it has been of considerable value to man. When unasked we take it upon ourselves to be their guardians, we the debtors owe it to birds to attend as fully as possible to their modest demands . . . like many things the keeping of birds in confinement sometimes leads to abuse. The resultant cruelty is seldom wilful, but is generally caused by thoughtlessness or ignorance. Readers of this book will have no excuse for any of this."

Many petshop owners have tame birds flying loose in their petshops with their wings cut back enough to prevent their escaping.

Mynah Birds in General

European Starlings, *Sturnus vulgaris,* are now spread almost worldwide. They devastate fruit crops like their cousins the Mynah Birds. Photo by W. Moreland. To the right is a prime example of a mature Greater Indian Hill Mynah, *Gracula religiosa intermedia.* Photo by Walsrode Vogelpark.

The Mynah Bird is a singing bird and, therefore, falls in the order Passeriformes. Within this order are about eighty different families and several hundred genera. The Mynah Bird belongs to the starling family, whose scientific name is Sturnidae. The keeping of Mynah Birds in captivity was for many years an exotic fancy until the advent of jet air freight after World War II created a worldwide market. India is the primary source for Mynah Birds; Thailand is the secondary source.

National Geographic writer Bart McDowell toured Simlipal National Park in 1970 on India's northeast coast with Mr. Saroj Raj Choudhury, Wildlife Conservation Of-

ficer in the state of Orissa. Soon they came upon some native tribesmen. "Soon we shall catch baby mynah birds. Good business," said clan leader Sambhu Dehuri. Mr. Choudhury explained: "The park promotes this work. If a mynah chick is taught to speak when it still takes food from your hand, it becomes a great mimic. The tribals climb high to the nests in tree hollows and take the mynah chicks very gently; they care for them well. They used to sell them to dealers, but now the park service buys them instead."

Did exporting three thousand Greater Hill Mynah birds a year deplete the Mynah population? "Not at all," answered Mr. Choudhury. "When robbed of chicks, the parent birds breed again. They can raise three clutches a year instead of one. We merely leave one clutch and take two—and the population remains constant. Mynahs, you may know, rarely breed in captivity." The tribesmen are delighted to sell to the government. "I used to get only half a rupee for a chick," said Mr. Dehuri, "now I get fifteen."

Similar methods are employed in Thailand. Collectors locate a Mynah nest during breeding season, mark the tree and then return to remove the fledglings just before the young birds are ready to leave the nest. The robust youngsters are easily hand-fed and quickly become completely tame. They are fed mainly boiled rice, diced fish and native cooked green vegetables. The Thai diet features hot red peppers which the baby birds apparently relish. One attendant can feed several hundred birds a day. The little babies crowd about during feeding time, raucous squeals issuing from their tiny throats. Baby Mynahs love hand-feeding and only reluctantly begin to eat from a dish or food cup. They clamber up the attendant's arms and perch on his head, shoulders and hands. As the birds are fed, they quiet down and drift away from their keeper.

Taken from the nest at three weeks, the birds are ready for overseas shipment within another three weeks. They are packed in long and wide but relatively flat crates. The sides of each crate are wire mesh, permitting the crates to be stacked in the luggage hold of the aircraft without suffocating the birds. The trip is not arduous though strange to the birds; most survive. When they arrive, for instance, in the United States, they are accustomed to human feeding and handling and, because of the relatively brief time spent in the baby bird farm and in transit, are unlikely to pick up many foreign words or phrases. There appears to be no noticeable difference between birds that come from Thailand and those that come from India.

The importer now takes over, initially hand-feeding the birds to make the transition as easy as possible for them. At the same time the importer can check the condition and health of each bird. Vitamin supplements and specially prepared Mynah pellets are usually provided at this point.

Since the Mynah Bird is a relative of the starling, its importation stimulated concern that it might become established as a wild bird in the United States with the same pestilential potential as the starling. In 1890 sixty starlings were released in New York's Central Park; a year later forty more were released. "From these one hundred birds," writes Oliver Austin, Jr., "have descended the millions of starlings that now occupy most of settled North America." Congregating in hordes on public buildings, the starlings showered their droppings on pedestrians and defaced the buildings. Their nightlong wheezing and chattering drove many city residents cuckoo, prompting as many different attempts at extermination as human ingenuity could devise.

Accordingly, when pet lovers began to import the Mynah Bird by the hundreds and then by the thousands, the Fish and Wildlife Service of the Interior Department swung into action. In April, 1952, Albert M. Day, Director of the Fish and Wildlife Service, proposed a blanket prohibition of all importation of starlings and Mynahs. He cited the fear that the birds would escape, propagate and become pests. As

13

evidence he noted that Mynah colonies had become established in Hawaii and in Vancouver, Canada—and that wild nesting activity had been discovered also in Los Angeles.

All-Pets Magazine lobbied vigorously against the proposed regulation, pointing out that the genera cited by the Fish and Wildlife Service were different from the commonly-kept talking Hill Mynah. With Congressional help they succeeded in getting the regulation altered to prohibit importation of all starlings and Mynahs except for the variety kept by pet fanciers. One telling argument was the obvious point that no one was going to buy a Mynah Bird, teach it to speak and then release it into the wild.

Thus, the regulation as finally adopted prohibited importation of birds of the family Sturnidae that are in the genus *Acridotheres* and the genus *Sturnus* "except for exhibition in zoological parks." Since the common pet Mynah is of the genus *Gracula,* continued importation was permitted. On October 13, 1952, the Fish and Wildlife Service confirmed this understanding in a letter to *All-Pets Magazine.* "The phraseology adopted," wrote asistant to the Director Frederick C. Lincoln, "was done deliberately to permit the importation of the talking Mynah known to ornithologists as *Gracula religiosa* . . ."

Sturnus pagodarum was once imported in huge quantities as housepets, but they never developed into great mimics like the other Mynahs. They have since been prohibited importation into most of the English-speaking countries of the world because of their voracious appetites for fruits on fruit trees, especially cherries. Photo from Kosmos Verlag.

Mynah
Bird
Species

Famous bird author Evelyn Miller claims to be able to teach any of the Mynah Bird species to mimic her. She put on many successful demonstrations and insists it is the fault of the teacher, not the bird, if a Mynah won't speak. Photo by Orlando, Three Lions.

To refresh your memory, recall that the Mynah Bird is a songbird of the order Passeriformes and a member of the family Sturnidae. The genus *Gracula* contains the only birds allowed to be imported. Therefore, let us turn our attention to the three members of this genus that are commonly available as pets. These are:

1.) The Greater Indian Hill Mynah (*Gracula religiosa intermedia*).

2.) The Lesser Indian Hill Mynah (*Gracula religiosa indica*).

3.) The Java Hill Mynah (*Gracula religiosa religiosa*).

"The observation of birds," writes ornithologist Alfred Newton, "has been from a very remote period a favorite pursuit among nearly all nations, and this observation has

To the left is a rare Rothschild Mynah, a cousin to the common Mynah Bird. Photo by Walsrode Vogelpark. The bird shown below is the Java Hill Mynah, *Gracula religiosa religiosa.*

To the right is the Yellow-faced Mynah, *Mino dumontii*, while below is the Golden-crested Mynah, *Ampeliceps coronatus*, from Burma and Thailand. These are very rare birds in captivity because they are banned from importation at the moment.

led by degrees to a study more or less framed on methodical principles, finally reaching the dignity of a science, and a study that has its votaries in almost all classes of the population of every civilized country."

The first namer of birds was Adam. "And out of the ground the Lord God formed every beast of the field, and every fowl of the air; and brought them unto Adam to see what he would call them: and whatsoever Adam called every living creature, that was the name thereof."

The first serious ornithologist whose writings we have is Aristotle (B.C. 385-322). Although he mentions more than one hundred and seventy birds, the account is disconnected and often scanty, especially in its description of individual types. Pliny the Elder, who died A.D. 70, expanded somewhat on Aristotle's work, but his classifications also were relatively crude. Albertus Magnus, who died A.D. 1282, wrote a twenty-six volume work, *De Animalibus*, of which book twenty-three is entitled *De Avibus*. In this volume, many birds appear for the first time in print, though the classifications are still rudimentary. Columbus's discovery of America stimulated many Europeans to undertake exploratory voyages to hitherto unknown parts of the world. Out of these voyages and the rising interest in scientific methodology arose the foundation of modern ornithology.

Generally acknowledged as the forerunner of modern treatises is John Ray's *Ornithologia*, published in 1676 and based upon his scientific partnership with Francis Willoughby who had died prematurely at age thirty-seven in 1672. In this work birds were grouped into two great divisions: land fowl and water fowl. The land fowl were subdivided into those which have a crooked beak and talons and those which have a straighter bill and claws. The Mynah bird would fall into the latter category, although British acquaintance with this bird did not really flower until the British were well established in India in the 1700's.

Nonetheless, the first scientific observation of the Mynah Bird—however unsophisticated—may have been recorded in John Ray's *Synopsis Methodica Avium* published in 1713. To this book was added a supplement by Petiver on the birds of Madras taken from pictures and information sent to him by Edward Buckley. Although I have not been able to examine this supplement to see if the Mynah Bird is included, it is the first attempt to catalogue the birds of any part of the British possessions in India.

The first fully authenticated classification of the Mynah Bird was done by Linnaeus in his celebrated *Systema Naturae*, edition 10 of 1758. In this work Linnaeus introduced the system of taxonomic differentiation that is still employed today, namely a binomial system in which the first term is the genus name and the second the particular species. In India the Hill Mynah Bird is commonly called a grackle; hence Linnaeus adopted the name *Gracula* for the genus description. The species name he chose was *religiosa*. He chose this name because he understood that the Hill Mynah was regarded as sacred to the Hindu deity Ram Deo. In this he was mistaken. As Jerdon points out in *Birds of India* (1862), the venerated bird is actually the common Mynah *(Acridotheres tristis)* and not the Hill Mynah *(Gracula religiosa)*. Nevertheless, Linnaeus's terminology was universally adopted and is what we use today.

Now let us note the distinctions among the subspecies of *Gracula religiosa*, for it is here that the pet fancier must make his choice.

Gracula religiosa intermedia: THE GREATER INDIAN HILL MYNAH

This bird is found in northeastern India and the Himalayas; it is also found in Burma, Thailand and other parts of southeast Asia. It shows great proficiency in learning to speak. A natural mimic, the Greater Hill Mynah Bird will imitate a variety of natural sounds in the wild.

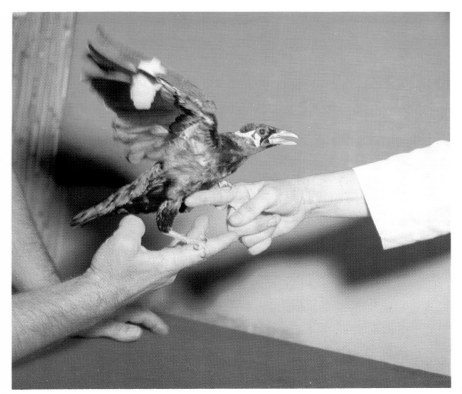

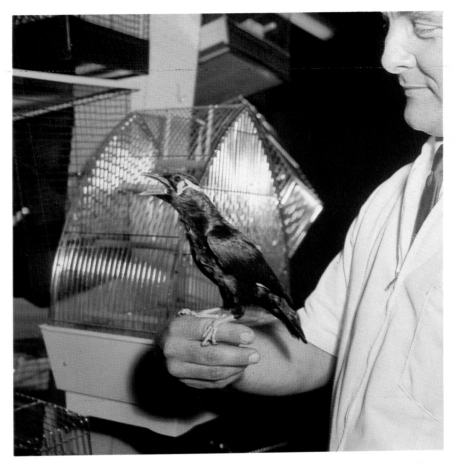

At the top of the facing page is a Mynah Bird without the white wing patches shown so obviously in the lower photo on the facing page. This splash of coloration is an "unofficial" characteristic of all the Mynahs. In the photo above, this bird is much larger, has a darker bill and, for its fully grown size, has a smaller head.

The Greater Hill Mynah Bird averages eleven inches in length. The plumage in the adult is black with an iridescent purple and green sheen. A band of white appears across the central area of the flight feathers. Head feathers are short with a velvety texture. The beak resembles Hallowe'en candy—bright orange fading to yellow on the tip. The tail is square and about three inches long. The feet and legs are yellow. The chief distinguishing features are the wattles—fleshy patches of bare skin that dangle over the nape of the neck. The wattles are bright yellow, a vivid contrast to the surrounding black feathers. They begin in the broad area below the eyes and extend backwards around the head, covering most of the lower facial area but not extending below the lower mandible. Narrowing at the nape of the neck, the wattles almost meet at the back of the head but are separated by a small triangle of velvety-black feathers. In fact, a noticeable central line extends from the crown to the nape; the velvety head-feathers seem to reach towards the dividing line. The wattle ends in a loose pendant lobe on the hind crown which dangles over the nape of the neck. The wattle is slightly interrupted behind and below the eyes by a small triangle of black feathers.

The wattle flaps develop slowly, being only slight bulbous swellings at the age of one year. Female wattles are smaller than those on the male. Aviary birds tend to develop larger flaps than cage birds. I would parenthetically mention here that since the wattles are an area of bare exposed flesh on the face and neck, they can predispose the Mynah Bird to catching a cold more readily than a bird whose head is fully feathered.

Gracula religiosa indica: THE LESSER INDIAN HILL MYNAH

This bird is found in southern India and in Sri Lanka

(Ceylon). It was once imported in large numbers as a substitute for the Greater Indian Hill Mynah Bird when the latter was quite expensive. However, it turned out to be a great disappointment as a pet because of its lack of steadiness and general inability to learn to talk.

In plumage the Lesser Indian Hill Mynah Bird resembles the Greater Indian Hill Mynah Bird but is noticeably smaller and more slender, rarely exceeding ten inches in length. In particular, the beak is far more slender and weaker, and the head is smaller. Apart from these distinctions, the wattles also assume a different configuration. Instead of nearly meeting at the back of the neck, they climb forwards toward the crown of the head in two bold U-shapes with a wide separation between them. Furthermore, instead of small feathered indentations in the wattles behind and below the eyes, the facial feathers completely interrupt them.

Gracula religiosa religiosa:
THE JAVA HILL MYNAH
This bird is found in southern Burma, Malaysia and on the Indonesian Islands of Sumatra, Java and Bali as well as in Borneo.

It is identical in coloration to *intermedia* and *indica* and grows to be eleven or twelve inches long including a tail two and one half inches long. It is the largest bird of the three, especially in the head and the thick beak, even though it is only one inch longer than *intermedia*. As in *indica* the wattle is divided behind the eye. Unlike *indica*, however, the Java Hill Mynah has flaps of wattle skin on the nape of the neck that are even larger in adulthood than those of *Gracula r. intermedia*.

This large heavy-bodied bird is the aristocrat of the pet Mynahs. Considerably more expensive than the Greater Indian Hill Mynah Bird, it is not consistently available. Nonetheless, fanciers consider it well worth the price and it finds a ready market when it is imported. Some *aficionados* consider the Java Hill Mynah Bird the best talker of all; others feel it is distinguished only by the questionable fact of having the loudest voice. If well taught, however, it speaks very clearly and is adept at learning to speak in the lower voice registers. When asked by an impressed observer where his Java Hill Mynah Bird acquired his beautiful resonant voice, a proud owner once replied, "His grandfather was a baritone too."

Sometimes confused with the Java Hill Mynah Bird is the even larger Nias Island Mynah Bird *(Gracula religiosa robusta)*, which is found in West Sumatra. A majestic bird, it reaches a length of fifteen inches in adulthood with a sizeable head and a thick beak. Under the right circumstances it can be the best talker of all, but it is hardly ever available.

With the thousands or even millions of Mynahs imported every year, the hand-fed and hand-reared youngsters hardly look anything like the mature wild Mynahs. On the facing page is a beautiful White-shouldered Starling, *Sturnus sinensis*. Photo by Harry Lacey.

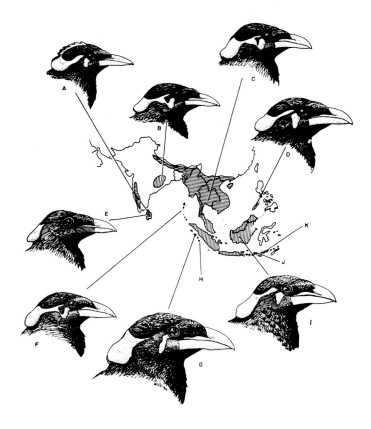

Selection

The map above, drawn by Dr. W.C. Dilger at Cornell, shows the distribution of (A) *Gracula religiosa indica;* (B) *G.r. peninsularis;* (C) *G.r. intermedia;* (D) *G.r. palawensis;* (E) *Gracula ptilogenys;* (F) *Gracula religiosa adamanensis;* (G) *G.r. robusta;* (H) *G.r. batuensis;* (I) *G.r. religiosa;* (J) *G.r. venerata;* and (K) *G.r. mertensi.* To the right: selecting a bird is very important. It must be alert, clean and healthy.

Now that you know how to distinguish the different available subspecies, you are ready to visit your neighborhood pet shop and look at a young specimen. It is recommended that you get out the Yellow Pages and identify from the advertisements several pet shops that specialize in imported pet birds. A few phone calls will allow you to discover if there are any young Mynahs in stock in your area or how soon one may be available from an importer.

Apart from selecting a bird that is alert, clean and healthy, it is of the utmost importance that you be able to identify the age of the bird you are acquiring. Ordinarily the bird you will be shown will be no more than six months

You can tell an intelligent, alert bird by the way it looks at you when you talk soothingly to it.

Mynah Birds should be alert, healthy and glossy.

old. The birds are shipped from abroad at two months of age and after three months in quarantine (required of all imported birds) they are available to pet shops at about five to six months old. The reason I emphasize the importance of acquiring as young a bird as possible is that the Mynah Bird acquires all its vocabulary of mimicry before its first birthday. To begin training a bird to talk even after it is eight months old is difficult; its thought and speech patterns may already be fixed.

There are two methods to identify the age of a young Mynah Bird. Just as young people have baby teeth that fall out and are replaced by adult teeth, so young Mynah Birds have baby feathers that fall out and are replaced by adult feathers. This is known as the adult molt and takes place between six and eight months from birth. The baby feathers are dull, grayish and somewhat straggly in appearance; the adult feathers are black with a green and purple sheen and lie smoothly in place. Therefore, if you want to be able to train your bird to talk, you must buy a bird that still has its baby feathers or is in the adult molt; it will look somewhat unattractive, but this is what you want!

Secondly, check the wattles. The more developed they are, the older the bird. Anne Keith offers the following guidelines: "The skin around the neck should be bare and fit tightly against the nape. There should be no signs of puffing on the back of the skin on the neck. A bird that shows signs of puffing on the skin on the nape is at least eight months old and although it will learn to talk, it will not be too good a talker. A bird that has flaps down the neck is over a year of age; and if it is not talking then, it will never say more than a few words."

By observing the wattles and the condition of the feathers, you will be able to make a sensible choice. As a final identifying characteristic you might check the beak which is more lightly colored in baby birds than in the adult Mynah Bird.

Two young Mynah Birds. They are easily identified by their size, the look about the face (bald) and the loss of their baby feathers. Photo by Louise van der Meid.

Check the wattles on your Mynah Bird. The more developed they are, the older the bird. The skin around the neck should fit tightly against the nape of the neck.

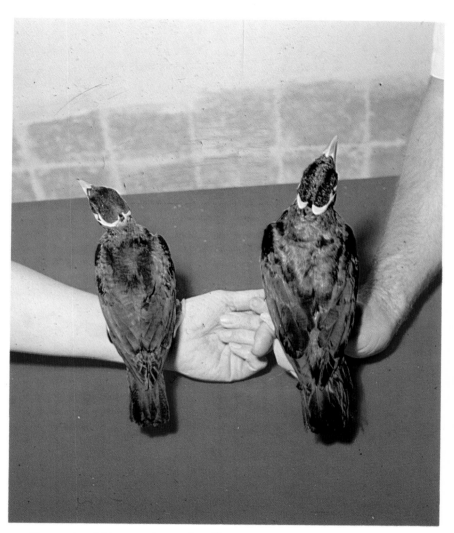

There should be no signs of puffing on the skin of the nape at the back of the head. A bird that shows puffing of the nape skin is at least eight months old. Flaps develop after one year of age.

Maintenance

You must depend upon your bird dealer or petshop owner to buy your bird and cage supplies. Don't buy a bird from just anyone. They might have a screaming old Mynah Bird they want to get rid of. Your dealer has a special Mynah Bird cage (above) and all the specialist supplies (right) you'll need, and he'll be there with professional advice. He has to know about Mynah Birds or he'd lose his own!

Before bringing your new pet home from the pet shop, prepare his new environment for him.

HOUSING

Unless you have an aviary, you will need a cage. Acquire the largest cage you can; the bird will appreciate it. Mynah Birds hop; they do not walk. Therefore, it is nice to have two perches so the bird can hop from one to the other. The pet shop owner will be able to advise you on choice of food-serving and water-drinking accessories. See if you can get a cage with a tray in the bottom that slides out for removing droppings and replacing litter. The less that cage-cleaning

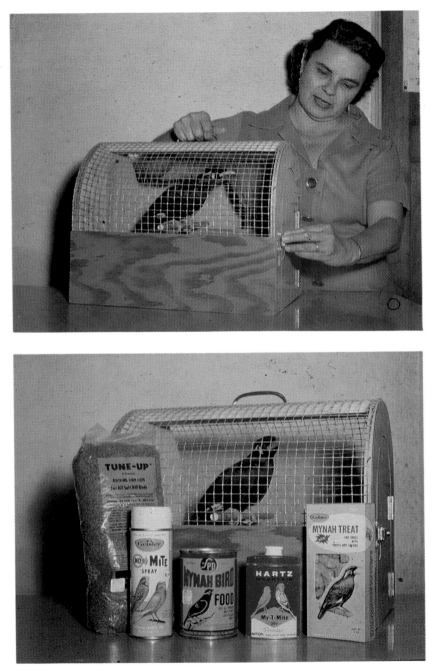

When you decide you want a Mynah Bird as a pet, you should consider the problems of bringing it home from the petshop. Many shops have small cat carriers (top, facing page) which they will rent to you for taking your pet home. Don't expect it *gratis* since it will be soiled by the bird's droppings and will have to be cleaned. You should also ask your pet dealer what the Mynah Bird has been eating and should buy a supply of everything he recommends (lower photo, facing page). Above all, get a good, large cage (above). The cage must be easily cleaned, have large spacing between the wires and assure that the droppings can easily fall through the bottom onto clean litter on the bottom tray. The tray must be easily removable for cleaning up.

activities disturb your bird, the better. Also a false-bottom tray that prevents the birds from pecking around in the litter and droppings is highly advisable.

Don't forget to keep the temperature steady. Sixty-five to seventy-five degrees Fahrenheit is best. Too much dry heat will overcome your bird; drafts and temperatures below fifty degrees invite illness. Some Mynahs sleep on the perch (make sure it is the proper size so the bird can get a proper grip) while others prefer sheltering under a newspaper or in a paper bag. One enterprising owner placed a deep shoe box with a hole cut in one end at the bottom of the cage; although his pet had always slept *au perch* before, he quickly adopted the shoe box as his bedroom. Give your pet a choice and he will choose what suits him. A rubber ball or a bell may be suspended in the cage as a plaything, but remember to keep all small swallowable foreign objects out of the cage.

The cage should be completely cleaned once a week. Unless you buy a cage with a heavy, long-lasting plated finish, it will eventually begin to rust. A high-quality cage is a good investment. If you can get stainless steel, so much the better. Remove the bird to a safe place and immerse the cage in a mixture of water and a mild cleaning agent to remove food particles and hardened droppings. Rinse thoroughly and wipe dry. The perches should also be cleaned carefully to avoid dirty feet and the problem of infection. Since your pet will probably clean its beak on the perch, you can understand the importance of keeping the perches clean. Scrape them with a knife and then use a perch brush available from a pet shop. Alternately the perches can be washed, but this alternative will necessitate two sets of perches as the washed perches must dry thoroughly to avoid chilling the bird's feet and causing rheumatism.

FEEDING
The feeding of Mynah Birds is not as difficult as it once

was because of the availability in your pet shop of Mynah pellets. These contain a balance of protein, dehydrated fruits, minerals and vitamins. It is in your interest and for the welfare of your pet as well to accustom it to a diet of Mynah pellets. The bird will be well nourished, its dropping will not be messy and you will have extra time to spend on taming, training and companionship. "The advent of mynah pellets," according to Hank Bates and Bob Busenbark, " is the most welcome innovation to bird fanciers since the cultivation of bird seeds." Another author notes that several of the Mynah Birds he owned "systematically eliminated every dietary item except mynah pellets; and they have always been healthier as a result." For variety, occasionally offer tiny pieces of apple, orange or banana, little bits of fat-free hamburger (raw), and peanut butter (which adds to glossiness of plumage). No seeds. The Mynah Bird has no crop and cannot digest them.

In summary, get your pet used to a predictable diet and stick to it. By using pellets, you will be freed from the job of cleaning up the normally splattered droppings of the fruit-eating Mynah Bird and you will not have to deal with the tendency of Mynah Birds to toss their food around the cage.

Do not give your bird food bits from your own meals. Watch your cigarettes. Mynah Birds are known to snatch a cigarette and swallow it, with dire consequences. The cure, by the way, is grapes and a drop of castor oil. Instruct the children: do not feed the bird. No weird food, table scraps or holiday treats. Keep the diet simple and repetitive, austere and nutritious.

Mynah Birds do not eat meals like people do. They peck all day long so let your bird eat as the spirit moves him. A pet owner who has mastered the problem of diet has allowed himself an opportunity for an aggravation- and disease-free experience with his pet.

A young bird loves the one who feeds it. In the upper photo, a mother Starling feeds its youngster. You have to imitate that behavior. The best way to a Mynah Bird's heart is through its stomach. Mynah Birds (facing page) love to eat, so offer them food from your hand. It will become a great training tool.

BATHING

Finally, the bird bath. Mynah Birds love to be clean and to preen. A daily morning bath is recommended so the bird will have plenty of daylight in which to dry and will also feel fresh for the day. A good time to do this is an hour before you clean the cage. The bathing dish (available from your pet shop) need contain no more than two inches of water. The bird will splash about and then groom itself afterwards. The cage should be cleaned every day and the droppings removed, although the total immersion cleansing need not occur more than once a week. Most people assume that birds love sunlight and that their pet would enjoy having its cage placed outside on a sunny day as it dries off from the bath. Be careful. Mynah Birds normally live in the perpetual twilight of dense jungles. Many agonizing deaths of Mynahs have been caused by overexposure to sunlight. By all means place the cage outside in the sun but only if you can arrange it so that the bird can retire into the shade if it wants to.

In conclusion, a properly equipped cage, a simple and regular diet and a daily bath will keep your bird in top condition without over-burdening you as the bird's keeper. If you attend conscientiously and habitually to these matters, you will be free to enjoy the provocative personality of the Mynah Bird.

Mynahs love to bathe and keep themselves clean if you'll just give them the chance. A large flat dish, not too deep, is just fine. But be careful—they splash and shake and cast water all around themselves . . . but they love it! Photo by Orlando, Three Lions.

Mynah Birds even love mealworms (upper right), but try to feed them in the feeding cup (above). Be sure the cup is locked in and can't be pushed out (lower photo, facing page) by a strong Mynah Bird. Their strength can fooı you!

Taming

As soon as your Mynah Bird has settled down in his new cage, introduce your hand into the cage very slowly and gently. Don't put your hand (above) over his head, as that makes him jumpy. If you really want to tame him quickly, have the flight feathers on one wing cut so he can't fly (right).

As you can see, not everyone is cut out to be a Mynah Bird owner. There is an old folk saying that tame owners make tame birds. If you are disorderly in your personal habits, I recommend that you do not acquire a pet Mynah Bird. It is rather inconsiderate to undertake the care, feeding and training of an imported bird if your own life is chaotic. This is why a pet bird is often a good selection for a young teen-ager who has a stable home environment, good sanitary habits and a steady disposition. The same is true for a mother whose children have grown up and left home. One of the most important ingredients in proper pet care is time. "Leisure to get to know the personality and qualities

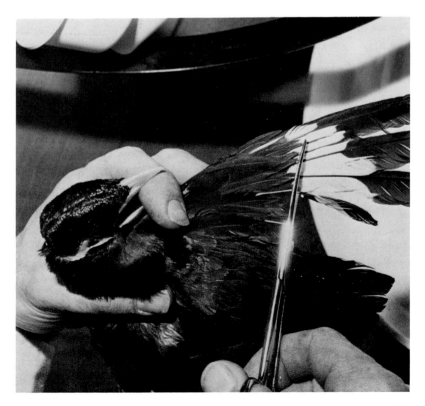

Handfeeding your Mynah Bird is probably the best way to make him tame (above). This Mynah Bird is eating vegetarian dog food! As soon as you select the Mynah Bird you want to buy, spread its wings and see if they have been cut (top, facing page). If the pet-shop owner will allow you, offer an over-ripe banana to a cage full of Mynahs and buy the first one that comes to feed from your hand, providing it is young and healthy.

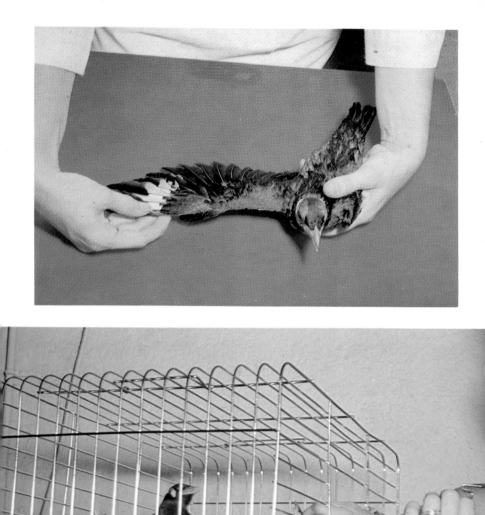

of a neighbor is as important in meeting birds," writes Grundy Steiner, "as in coming to know one's fellow man."

A Mynah Bird is not a good choice for therapy for a lonely distraught person. You will only end up with a distressed miserable bird. Be honest with yourself; if you don't have the temperament to care for yourself properly, why take on a pet bird as well? Think this matter over carefully because, regardless of how you feel, the bird of necessity requires devoted daily attention.

Once the care routine is established and the bird is accustomed to its new home, it is time to develop a more personal relationship with it. Since you are in control, the bird will respond to your cues. Be patient. Be gentle. Be calm. Remember how huge and powerful a human being appears to a bird. Be a courteous giant. Take care not to alarm your pet and if you have an impish teasing nature keep it under control. Grabbing the bird bodily, pulling your finger away as the bird hops on, slapping the cage or shouting in frustration can develop the dread retaliatory personality, resulting in unpredictable attacks from the Mynah Bird's piercing claws and pounding beak. Mynah Birds are too simple to understand the concept of forgiveness; once you are branded as an enemy the bird will attack on sight with instinctive fury. One Mynah Bird, for instance, used to attack all people with crew cuts because it had once been badly mistreated by a flat-topped human being.

Now then, King Kong, your goal is to turn your pet into a trusting Fay Wray so that it would gladly perch on your shoulder while you climb the Empire State Building. Here is how to begin: visualize in your mind the result you want to achieve—namely, the bird perching cheerfully on your shoulder or outstretched finger. Make it seem like a pleasant dream to your pet. Leave the room in semi-darkness and open the cage door offering your hand, perhaps with a tiny piece of fruit in it. If you have treated your pet well in its initial days with you, it may hop right on! Otherwise nudge the bird gently in the chest with your forefinger held sideways. Forced backwards it will probably flutter up and light on your hand. After a few days of this kind of unpressured practice, your bird will come to enjoy your companionship and look forward to your visit and the prospect of spending some time outside the cage. As the bird flight-tests the room, make sure the curtains are drawn so it doesn't crash into a window.

Your tone of voice is very important. In the initial pre-taming days strive to develop a reassuring way of talking to your pet. Be sweet, kind, affectionate. Speak softly with a cooing tenderness. Children have a natural facility for training birds as they have innocent trusting natures. A girl of eight or nine is an ideal companion for a baby bird. I might mention here that since children have limited vocabularies they have also proven to be very good at teaching birds to talk. I suggest that you learn a lesson from the great plant breeder, Luther Burbank. He loved plants and saw them as his dearest friends. In talking to his plants he reassured them of his love. His patience and dedication paid off. In one celebrated case, he bred a cactus without prickles. "While I was conducting experiments to make spineless cacti," he once said, "I often talked to the plants to create a vibration of love. You have nothing to fear, I would tell them. You don't need your defensive thorns. I will protect you."

No pet is ever going to please its master completely, but if you love your pet, you will receive much affection in return. One experienced Mynah Bird owner reported in the August, 1979 issue of *American Cage-Bird Magazine:* "I can't imagine how I ever got along without his company. He may drive some of my family and friends nuts with his squawks, screeches, rantings and ravings, but to me his special sounds have been and will always be music to my ears."

Once your Mynah Bird is tame, you can train him to imitate your voice by constantly repeating the same word over and over again (above). Never keep two Mynah Birds in the same cage during a training lesson (top, facing page). Once the bird repeats the word or phrase correctly, reward him with fruit cocktail or any other favorite he might have.

Talking

Mynah Birds don't talk; they mimic your voice or the voice of the one who trains them.

Mynah Birds are intelligent, curious and, of course, superb mimics. "To assume some counterpart to human intelligence and the human spirit in a creature that apparently possesses an equivalent of speech is very natural," writes Grundy Steiner, "and the behavior patterns of many birds create impressions of remarkable intelligence ..." Raconteur Michael Baselici cites a case in point. He tells of one Mynah Bird that predicted the Superbowl victor seven years in a row. The eighth year the bird picked Minnesota over Miami by seven points. "Of course, I bet on Minnesota and got seven points to boot," Baselici recalls. "Miami won by twenty-four."

Older birds, like the one shown above, are difficult to train. They must be as young as the bird on the facing page, where the bald face, tight wattles and juvenile plumage indicate that this Mynah Bird is well under six months of age.

Pliny the Elder, who lived at the time of Christ, alludes to the starlings which were trained for the amusement of the young Caesars; they spoke both Latin and Greek. In *Henry IV,* Part I, Hotspur found a way to get around the injunction never to mention Mortimer: teaching a friendly starling to utter the name with merciless repetition.

He said, he would not ransom Mortimer;
Forbade my tongue to speak of Mortimer;
But I will find him when he lies asleep,
And in his ear I'll holloa, *'Mortimer!'*
Nay, I'll have a *starling* shall be taught to speak
Nothing but 'Mortimer,' and give it him,
To keep his anger still in motion.

When M. Girardin visited his friend M. Thirel in Paris, he was astonished to hear a starling utter a dozen consecutive sentences with an intonation indistinguishable from a French aristocrat. When the bell rang for mass, the same bird called to its mistress by name, "Mademoiselle, are you going to mass? Take your book and return quickly, and give your naughty bird something to eat." (I apologize for my translation: the bird spoke high-society French).

These examples should indicate the depth of the Mynah Bird's capability to talk, definitely exceeding that of any parrot. Mynah Birds will imitate anything that they hear fairly regularly. Therefore, if you don't want your bird to become a catch-all of household sounds, you must control its auditory environment during the decisive learning period from the age of six months to a year. The bird will imitate what it hears—and if it hears something often enough you can be fairly sure that it will become part of its repertoire. For instance, a Mynah Bird that is trained by a child will soon come to imitate the child's voice. When the child grows older and its voice deepens, the Mynah Bird will continue to imitate the higher pitch and inflection it originally heard!

Mynah Birds do not have to be taught to talk—they are natural mimics. In the wild they imitate the calls of other birds and will do the same in an aviary. Therefore, it is up to you to decide if you want to have any control over the direction this natural inclination takes. The earlier you begin voice training the better. Once the bird is a year old, it will rarely learn new words or phrases, especially if it has not acquired the habit of accepting human instruction earlier.

Choose the words you wish the bird to learn and repeat them slowly over and over for about fifteen minutes a day—no more. You can use a pre-programmed training record or a tape recorder if you wish. Be patient. You may be surprised at how fast your bird learns. Don't forget that it can also imitate a ringing telephone, a running faucet, a barking dog, a screeching door, etc. It is inadvisable to teach your pet to whistle unless you have a soundproof room in which to put the bird. On the other hand, if you wish you can probably teach your pet to whistle some simple tunes. Sure hope you like hearing them! Whistling birds, by the way, tend to show a diminished interest in learning to talk.

Enunciate clearly. Persevere. Remember, the first few words are the hardest to teach. Thereafter the bird will learn rapidly, and its proficiency will grow. Go slowly because the Mynah Bird will tend to speak faster than you do when it repeats its lessons. Allow a noticeable pause between repetitions of a phrase. Otherwise the bird may begin repeating the phrase in rapid succession.

As with taming, a semi-darkened room will tend to calm the bird. To absorb the bird's attention fully, observe its habits and pick a time of day when it is relatively idle and unoccupied with bathing, preening or feeding. Twenty minutes at a time is plenty. The first lessons may take up to a month to learn. Two weeks is rapid, indeed. Regular

Tame and train your bird in a semi-darkened room so the Mynah Bird will give you all its attention and not be diverted by shadows or external movements. Mynah Birds are extremely alert and sensitive to movements.

Mynahs soon become friends of the household, but their droppings are very loose, so whatever you do, don't encourage them to sit on your head!

Mynahs soon become friends of the household, but their droppings are very loose, so whatever you do, don't encourage them to sit on your head!

orderly instruction will achieve the result you desire. Frequent reviews of past learning are desirable so vocabulary does not lapse.

Mynah Birds are capable of developing repertoires of hundreds of words and phrases. Their intelligence is really remarkable. Only in a rare case does a diligent pet owner approach the full potential of these birds.

Should you ever want to eliminate an undesirable squawking or whistling habit, cover the cage with a dark cloth or remove the bird and cage into a darkened room whenever the undesirable outburst begins. The bird in time will make the connection. This is a proven technique though it may take a couple of weeks of calm deliberate discipline to achieve the result.

A trio of Golden-crested Mynahs on the facing page. Photo by Louise van der Meid. Above is a pair of Shining Starlings building a nest. They are sometimes sold as Red-eyed Mynahs, but they are no longer available since all imports from Australia and New Guinea have ceased. Photo by R. Garstone.

Coming home! If you bought the right cage, you can cover it with a blanket and move it from the shop into your car. The Mynah Bird (facing page) has strong grasping feet and he won't fall off the perch as you bounce him around for a few minutes. Photo by Harry Lacey.

Questions
and
Answers

70

Budgerigars (sometimes called parakeets), shown above, are also excellent pets and good talkers. The Fischer's Lovebird shown on the facing page is also a great pet bird that mimics sounds. Photos by Kwast and Aaron Norman.

(The following series of questions and answers is based upon an interview between the author and Dr. Matthew Vriends in January, 1980 at the T.F.H. offices in Neptune, New Jersey).

Which birds are most commonly kept in the home or aviary?
Most common are canaries, budgerigars, certain finches (e.g., the zebra finch), cockatoos and cockatiels. Certain strains developed by breeders are also popular such as society finches.

Dr. Pastore, an animal psychologist, trains canaries to act according to predetermined stimuli. On the facing page: a great talking parrot is the rare Lesser Sulphur-crested Cockatoo. Photo by World-wide.

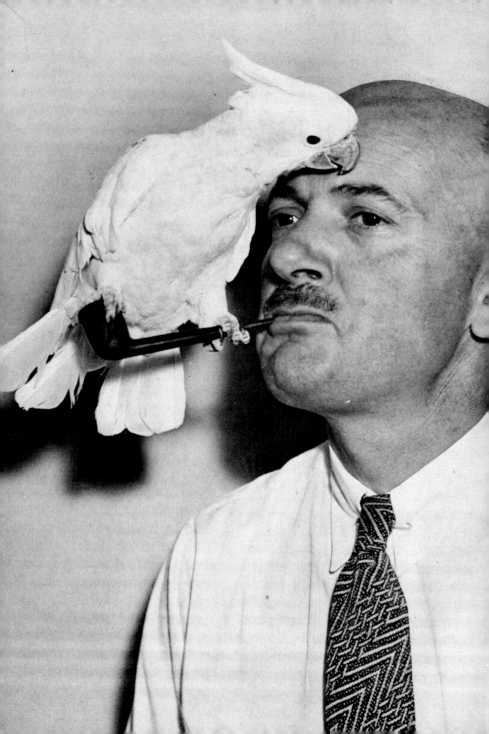

Your petshop should recommend that you buy a bird net in order to catch your Mynah Bird when he flies around the house and doesn't want to get back into the cage when you want him to (facing page, top). On the bottom of the facing page, a typical louse and mite spray requires a bit of cooperation to get the spray under the wings of the Mynah bird where the lice take refuge. Special dried foods, made just for Mynah Birds, are available, and your petshop can supply them.

What are the advantages or disadvantages or keeping a Mynah Bird as opposed to a canary, a cockatoo, a cockatiel or a budgerigar?

As to its disadvantages, the Mynah Bird requires quite a bit of nursing and attention because the droppings are very watery. Therefore, the cage must be cleaned at least once a day. In order to keep them healthy, these birds require quite a variety of food. Although a ready-to-serve Mynah Bird food is on the market, it is necessary also to feed the bird fruits and berries. The Mynah Bird is omnivorous, preferring fruit and insects. It rarely eats seeds. A Mynah Bird on an exclusive seed diet would die in a couple of days. In general one needs to be an experienced aviculturist to maintain a Mynah Bird. The budgerigar, for example, is a seed-eater. The pet owner can go to the pet shop, buy a packet of seed, and that's it. Not so with the omnivorous Mynah. The Mynah Bird requires daily care including cleaning the cage. It likes an occasional bath in soft rain. In general, the Mynah Bird is more demanding than other pet birds.

On the other hand, there are advantages to keeping a Mynah Bird. They are extremely funny birds in the way they act and jump around. They also are extremely good imitators, which can be a disadvantage if the bird is trained improperly. One Mynah Bird I once owned began to imitate the cough of my grandfather who was in terminal illness. They will even imitate squeaky doors. Any sound the bird hears is a possibility for mimicry. House noises and other bird calls are easily picked up. On the other hand, they are very teachable. You can teach a Mynah Bird how to talk, which is in itself—for an aviculturist, at least—an interesting point. I have known Mynah Birds which could be taught to catch small pieces of apple in their beaks. In general the Mynah Bird is more sophisticated than a budgerigar. However it is wise not to teach a Mynah Bird circus tricks such as ringing a bell or running up and down a ladder. The bird possesses a certan dignity that makes it balk at such training.

Which species of Mynah would you recommend to the prospective pet owner?

This is a very difficult question. In my own experience the Greater Mynah imitated bird songs in an aviary without any training and also ate out of my hand. I suggest that you give them big birds as company in an aviary. They will quickly kill canaries or budgerigars, for Mynah Birds are very aggressive. Especially in the breeding season, if you have a pair of Mynah Birds, house them in a separate aviary because they will kill practically any bird that comes in sight. The Mynah Bird is vicious in defending its territory. I think that the Greater Mynah Bird is *the* pet.

Are there any special health problems peculiar to the Mynah Bird?

Soft-billed birds such as the Mynah Bird are susceptible to all kinds of illnesses, especially colds. I mention this because 90% of birds are kept indoors in a cage where they are very susceptible to drafts. If you overfeed them, they will get diarrhea and will dehydrate. The main thing to look for is whether or not the bird keeps its feathers nice and straight in a line. As long as the feathers are not puffed up, everything is most likely in order. If the bird is found sitting in a corner with its head tucked under a wing and shivering, it is ill.

Since a Mynah Bird is quite expensive in the United States, it is wise to have available the address of a veterinarian who is familiar with avian diseases. You may wish to write to a local bird club to find out which veterinarians would be available in case of an emergency. It is well worth the cost of a visit to the veterinarian to protect an expensive bird. Therefore, it is necessary to set aside some money for health care. It is unwise to exhaust com-

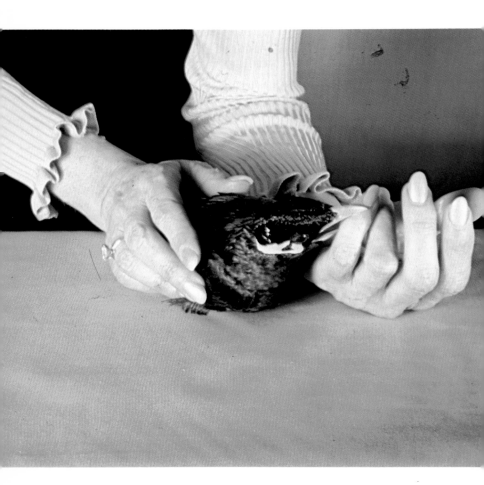

You should learn to handle your Mynah Bird and overcome the fear that most people have for birds. A Mynah Bird is a soft-billed bird, and his bite can just pinch without usually breaking the skin.

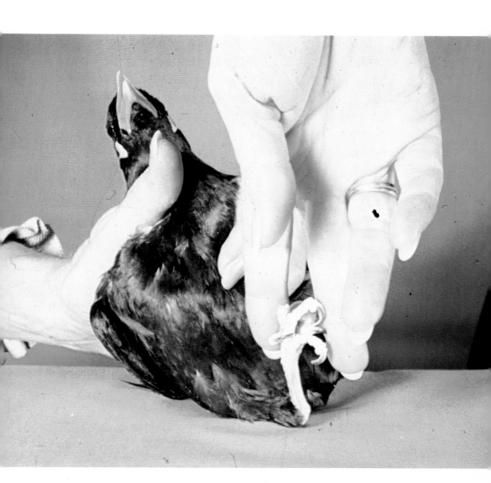

You'll have to learn to handle your Mynah Bird in all positions in order to cut his nails or to examine him closely. Practice gently, don't squeeze, but be firm.

pletely your budget on buying the bird, housing and feeding it, and allow no money for medical attention. Trying to scrimp on health care is indeed a foolish economy.

Because the birds are so extremely expensive, the owner automatically has to consult a veterinarian if the bird comes down with more than a common cold. If the problem is simply a common cold, the bird needs warmth—perhaps in a hospital cage—and an environment free of drafts. Drafts are the biggest killers of birds in captivity. What is a brisk breeze to a person may be a murderous gale to a small bird. If you have to treat a Mynah Bird for illness, do not deprive him of food and water. Proper treatment and medication can fail if the diet is not maintained during convalescence.

How would you describe the personality of the Mynah Bird?
He is very aggressive, especially during breeding season. He is very alert and also very nosy. Like a little child, he must know everything that is going on. Talking or mimicry come from this habit of intense curiosity about everything in his environment. He is also, as mentioned before, very aggressive to small birds in an aviary.

Are Mynah Birds peaceable or contentious as compared to other pet birds?
The Mynah Bird will become very friendly to the man or woman who cares for it and towards its keeper will be extremely tame and unaggressive. A tame bird can be handled properly even by a small child, but the bird must be personally familiar with the child first. A Mynah Bird has a very good "memory." I have come across quite a few birds that dislike, for example, all male human beings because a man once mistreated them. Be wary. Their beaks are very sharp, although they rarely aim for the face. Nonetheless, I

would point out the following: all starlings are fascinated by anything that shines and glistens. A couple of European species related to the Mynah Bird, for example, are known for collecting glittering objects such as rings and shiny buttons. Although it is not a scientifically verified fact, it is possible that a glint in the eye could attract the attention of a Mynah Bird. If the eye belongs to a stranger or a feared individual, a serious injury might occur. If people unfamiliar with your Mynah Bird come to visit, make sure they keep their distance. Children love to touch and poke. Use common sense and keep them away from your pet Mynah Bird until you can acclimate the bird to their presence.

Please describe two or three differing viewpoints on the proper care of the Mynah Bird.

I don't think there is a definitive method. Clean the cage daily; give them a variety of food. I used to give them mice litters during the breeding season. They loved it. A little bit of minced raw meat is also eagerly eaten as a rule. The acceptability of a particular food can depend on the individual bird. Thus, it is important to be flexible and observant. Each bird is an individual with its own feelings and character. I have seen mean Mynah Birds; I have seen gentle Mynah Birds. Some are very fond of dry foods; others prefer oranges and bananas. Therefore, I suggest that you try out various foods. If your bird refuses a particular item, it is best to stop offering it. Individual Mynah Birds can differ in accepting or rejecting a particular food. I usually advise asking the pet shop owner what type of food they were given before importation and what he has been feeding them. If the diet is not satisfactory to you, increase the quality of the food.

Would you consider the Mynah Bird a superior talking bird to the African Grey Parrot?

Yes, obviously. The African Grey is somewhat overrated.

African Gray Parrots are probably over-rated as the world's greatest talkers, but they are cleaner and easier to have running loose about the house. Photo by Dr. Herbert R. Axelrod.

The Mynah Bird will become very friendly to the one who feeds and cares for it. Once that relationship is established, the Mynah Bird will allow that person to handle it in almost any way.

Depending on the individual bird, the Mynah Bird is definitely as good a talker as the African Grey and, most likely, better. Again, it depends on the bird. Overall, the Mynah Bird is a superior mimic to the African Grey Parrot.

In your opinion, what is the best way to train a talking bird?

Have a lot of patience. It is absolutely necessary to start with a young bird. Don't be surprised if it takes you six to eight months or longer. Repeat the same word or phrase over and over. Use simple words: 'hello,' ' baby,' the bird's name, etc. After preliminary training, you may wish to employ a tape recorder. Get a blank tape and record repetitively the phrase or phrases you wish the bird to mimic. When you are busy elsewhere, put the tape recorder in the room with the bird. It will be an effective silent teacher.

Voice training is best in the morning when the bird is alert. Late in the afternoon the bird is likely to be sleepy and uninterested. Be patient. Do not move on to another word or phrase until the first one is imitated properly. There is no harm in holding the bird's attention by offering him a special food treat after the instruction is completed—as a reward for his cooperation. But, please, no more than fifteen minutes a day or boredom sets in.

How do Mynah Birds get along with other birds in a mixed aviary?

Outside of the breeding season this arrangement is possible if you have a well-planted large garden aviary that permits the other birds to hide or get away. During breeding season if you have a pair of Mynah Birds they are best isolated in a small aviary at least nine or ten feet long and six feet high. The pair will do nicely without any other birds around. This arrangement, indeed, will allow them the best opportunity for nesting. I am hesitant, in general, to recommend Mynah Birds for a mixed aviary, except with large birds such as pheasants. Never mix them with smaller birds, as they will eat them.

Does the Mynah Bird have any difficulty in adapting to the climate of the temperate zone?

No. In the colder states from the Canadian border south to the Mason-Dixon line Mynah Birds can be kept even in winter. In India many wild birds live in high frigid altitudes during the winter, but since we cannot nourish and exercise them as well as in the wild, it is best during the winter to keep them indoors or in a frost-free sheltered part of the aviary. Although a Mynah Bird will play and jump in the snow on a sunny winter day, an adequate shelter connected with the garden aviary is essential. On a sunny cold day, you can let the bird out a little, but to be on the safe side keep it indoors in a closed cage. This is a matter for judgment. Be cautious if you are inexperienced or the bird is facing its first winter outside the tropics.

In general give the bird lots of room and keep it clean. In the colder states, if you do not have a garden aviary with a shelter, leave the bird indoors. It is best not to house your bird in the kitchen as the smells can sometimes be disagreeable to the delicate appetite of the Mynah Bird and sicken it. Also kitchen temperatures can vary widely. Flinging open a window to cool apple pies that have just come from a hot oven can wreak havoc on a pet bird.

Cleanliness, of course, has a lot to do with the disposition of all clean animals and the Mynah Bird is no exception. He loves to bathe, but the procedure can be disastrous if proper precautions are not taken, with the result that the entire cage and surroundings become sopping wet. Give him plenty of room for his bath. This is better than having to face a condition where droppings begin to stick to the plumage, inviting disease.

If your Mynah Bird is allowed the freedom of the house (top, facing page), you must ensure that he cannot fly into hot or poisonous liquids. In the lower photo on the facing page, you can see the type of droppings and how they may stain or damage furniture. If you must carry your Mynah Bird, hold your hand under him. The same is true of them flying onto your sleeve, where their claws (see above) may get tangled in soft material and cause them to break a leg or tear your sweater as they fly away.

At one time the Mynah Bird had a reputation for a wet, sloppy stool. What are your dietary recommendations?

Because the Mynah Bird eats a lot of fruit, the droppings will naturally tend to be watery. There is not much you can do about it. They are very fond, for instance, of raisins, especially if soaked overnight. This is a nice treat, by the way, after talking lessons.

Is there any danger that escaped Mynahs might become pests like their family relation, the starling?

No, because in the United States there is not enough food available. If not caught, an escaped bird will most likely die within a couple of days. Also, a bird that has been in captivity for quite a while loses all sense of danger and will be easy prey for a cat or other animal.

To prevent escape, do you recommend clipping, stripping or an alternative method?

When a bird is hand-tamed, neither is necessary. In my book clipping wings is unnecessary if you have your bird trained. When you begin your lessons, keep the doors and windows locked and the curtains drawn. Otherwise the bird may slam into the glass and break its neck or wings. The Mynah Bird is not a big flyer. If your bird seems wild, you may want to clip one wing, but most imported birds are quite tame. In general I am against wing-clipping because the bird has already had to endure the rigors of transportation to a new continent. Therefore, it deserves a little extra consideration. If treated well, it will be hand-tamed within a week, rendering clipping unnecessary. Young birds are very affectionate and there is no sound reason to make the little creature feel completely helpless. Once the bird has had a couple of days to become acclimated to its new home, begin to speak friendly words to it. After three months in a quarantine station, the bird will welcome personal attention from you and begin to enjoy its permanent home.

Not everyone is in favor of clipping a Mynah's wing, but if the procedure is performed it *must* be done carefully.

Is it realistic for the average pet owner to aspire to show his Mynah Bird?

I don't see any harm, especially if it is tame. Showing your bird will increase your own interest in bird life and the increased attention the bird receives can only redound to its benefit. Even if you have previous experience caring for a living creature, you may find that preparing a bird for a showing will reveal the extent of your own regard and love for life.

Are some birds cleaner than others? Where does the Mynah Bird fit in?

He is a messmaker. If he is looking for a particular item, he may toss the food in his eating cup around. Some people consider the Mynah Bird a poor pet for this reason. The patient owner, however, understands that there may be a sound reason for such behavior. Any bird in the wild is its own doctor. If there is a lack of a certain food, the bird will launch a search for this particular food. He will in captivity spill his food for the same reason.

An Eastern Rosella Parrot and a Cockatiel with its crest raised. Cockatiels are extremely popular pets.

Although most Mynahs are gentle birds, it is safer never to trust one too close to your face. The sharply pointed bill could cause an accidental injury. Photo by Dr. Herbert R. Axelrod.

Mynahs that are bored might easily take their food and spit it all around. If you feed them outside their cage, take that into consideration.

On the other hand, food splattering may also be a game for a bored pet. Alert and curious, he may purposely misbehave just to see what happens. If the bird is not given daily attention (talking to him, allowing him to fly free in the room for a couple of hours), he will be bored stiff and try various means to get attention. He may call monotonously and repeatedly or flap his wings wildly. A moderate recreation program is wise for all pet birds.

Can Mynahs be bred successfully in captivity? Which species?
This is possible with the three species from India, especially if they are kept in a well-planted aviary without any companions.

Apart from breeding, is there any reason to prefer a male Mynah for a pet as opposed to a female Mynah?
No. This is a fairy tale. Actually it depends on the individual bird and the teacher, not the sex of the bird.

Mynah Birds do have eyelids. This picture was taken with a fast strobe light which stopped the eyelid in the middle of a wink.